52 WAYS TO SIMPLIFY YOUR LIFE

Steve Woodworth

OLIVER
NELSON

THOMAS NELSON PUBLISHERS
Nashville

To my wife, Tricia—thou excellest them all!
And to our friends, Jerome and Dorothy—fellow
pilgrims on the narrow way

Published in Nashville, Tennessee, by Oliver-Nelson Books, a division of Thomas Nelson, Inc., Publishers, and distributed in Canada by Lawson Falle, Ltd., Cambridge, Ontario.

The Bible version used in this publication is THE NEW KING JAMES VERSION. Copyright © 1979, 1980, 1982, Thomas Nelson, Inc., Publishers.

Scripture quotation noted NASB is from the New American Standard Bible, © 1960, 1962, 1963, 1968, 1971, 1972, 1973, 1975, 1977 by The Lockman Foundation. Used by permission.

Printed in the United States of America.

Library of Congress Cataloging-in-Publication Data
Woodworth, Steve, 1956–
    52 ways to simplify your life / Steve Woodworth.
        p.   cm.
    ISBN 0-8407-9668-4 (pbk.)
    1. Conduct of life.   I. Title.   II. Title: Fifty-two ways to simplify your life.
    BJ1581.2.W675 1993
    158′.1—dc20   92-41823
                                                                  CIP

            1   2   3   4   5   6 — 98   97   96   95   94   93

◼️ Contents

Cultivate Your Spirit

Make Peace with Your Enemies

Simplify Your Finances

Do It Yourself

Don't Do It Yourself

■■ Introduction

*Our life is frittered away by detail. An honest man
has hardly need to count more than his ten fingers,
or in extreme cases he may add his ten toes, and
lump the rest. Simplicity, simplicity, simplicity!*
—Henry David Thoreau

Our lives get more complex every day. How many of us haven't longed to drop out altogether? We read about men and women who have left high-paying careers and moved to the country to find a higher quality of life, and something tugs at all of us to get out, to return to a simpler life-style.

Even the little things in our lives are burdensome. Most of us still can't figure out how to record a show on the VCR. By the time we learn how to use it, it will be obsolete!

The volume of choices we face is overwhelming. There are fifty-three channels on our TV cable system, forty kinds of soap to wash our dishes, and hundreds of styles of clothing to choose from.

We're bombarded with information. The average person sees several thousand advertising messages every day. There are more words in the average Sunday newspaper than in the entire Bible.

Information changes so quickly that an encyclopedia is out of date by the time it's printed.

I have good news. There is a way out of this complexity short of moving to the backwoods in Maine. It's possible to simplify our lives. It's possible to find an island of peace in the midst of this frantic world. People have always faced this issue. It's harder today than it's ever been, but the principles passed down from earlier generations still work.

This book offers practical information. It's not a philosophical treatise about simplicity. I'm a businessman, with all the demands of balancing family, church, career, and community. My wife and I have worked hard for the last ten years to simplify our lives. Through trial and error, we've had some success. The suggestions in this book have worked for us.

Most of the ideas are simple. (I wouldn't be very consistent if I gave complex suggestions to simplify your life!) But just because the ideas are simple doesn't mean they're all easy to incorporate into your life. Complexity is addicting. Slowing down, even though you desire it, is a challenge. If you have eyes to see the problem and the will to make changes, the suggestions here will work for you. Once you get started, the joy of a simpler life will be all the motivation you need to keep going. May you find greater peace and joy than you ever thought possible!

Develop Habits of Rest and Reflection

The driven person can never lead a simple life.
Liberating yourself from drivenness is the
essential first step.

1 ∷ Get Enough Sleep

Fatigue makes cowards of us all.
—Vince Lombardi

Background Some experts now believe that adults need between eight and ten hours of sleep per night. The average adult gets seven hours.

Think about the days before electric lights and television. People had little to do after dark. Families sat near the fire and talked. I'm sure it didn't take long to get sleepy. Most people were in bed a few hours after sundown. The body's rhythms were therefore dictated by the length of the day. In the summer, they would be up early and work hard until late at night. But for most of the year, eight to ten hours were probably a normal night's sleep.

Think about what happens to you on vacation. That can indicate what your body is trying to tell you. I usually continue my normal sleeping pattern the first few days. By the fourth or fifth day, I sleep an extra hour or two. If it's a long vacation, I sleep ten hours at night and even take a nap at midday by the second week.

If our bodies really do need eight to ten hours of sleep, how do we get by on seven? We make up the difference with adrenaline. But we pay the price in fatigue and reduced effectiveness.

Action If you are tired most of the time, there is only one solution: sleep more. If this applies to you, getting more sleep is the first step toward simplifying your life.

That's easier said than done, I know. How can you afford to sleep more since you have so much to do? Throughout the rest of this book, the other 51 ways should show you how to find more time. But begin now to give yourself permission to sleep. Many of us feel guilty about sleeping. That's silly. Our bodies are designed to need sleep, just as we need air and water. We don't feel guilty taking the air and water we need.

For those of us on a job schedule, it's usually not possible to sleep later in the morning. We must go to bed earlier. If you watch TV in the evenings, turn it off and allow your mind to wind down earlier. Television and electric lights artificially stimulate us. Long after earlier generations would have been in bed, we are in front of the TV, unaware that the body is telling us it's tired. Try taking a hot bath to help you relax. If you are married, you and your spouse can rub each other's back in bed.

Try going to bed fifteen minutes earlier. If it works, add another fifteen minutes. Consider whether you have more energy the next day. You may miss out on a chunk of time each day, but you'll more than make up for it in increased energy!

2 ∷ Have a Rest Day

The Sabbath was made for man.

—Mark 2:27

Background If you are a Christian or a Jew, you know the concept of a Sabbath. God decreed that everyone must rest one day each week. He considered it so important that He made it one of the Ten Commandments. No work could be done on the Sabbath.

Why did God establish a rest day? Because it's good for us. It fits our natural rhythms. Our bodies need times of rest. Constant activity, day after day with no breaks, is like music without any rests.

It's an established medical fact that people with Type A personalities, those who have trouble resting, have more heart attacks, high blood pressure, ulcers, and a host of other problems.

We also benefit spiritually from a rest day because it's an act of faith to stop working. We have faith that there is One who will take care of us, that we needn't strive seven days a week. We say, "God, I trust You with the consequences of stopping to rest today."

Action It doesn't matter what day you choose to rest; it's just important that you take off a day. For most of us, Sunday is a good day. We work five days for an employer, Saturday is the day we catch up on personal business, and Sunday is the most natural day to take it easy.

Starting this habit takes discipline. I began it two years ago when I had a full-time job and was consulting for extra income. I could do my consulting work at home, and I usually chose Sunday to do it. I was making good money, but I was increasingly stressed. I knew I had to change something. My quality of life was deteriorating rapidly.

I made a commitment to try to have a rest day.

At first, I was obsessed on Sunday morning with thoughts of all I could achieve that day. I kept reminding myself that it was my day to rest, and I asked God to help me trust Him with my unfinished work. After church, I would read, take a nap, take a walk with Tricia, go on an outing at the beach, help cook a nice meal—anything that was relaxing.

Now, this habit is one of the most rewarding disciplines of my life. I still find time to do occasional consulting on a day other than Sunday. In fact, I don't feel I have lost any time. My outlook on life is much more focused, my energy is higher, and I have learned a vital lesson about my natural rhythms. I have lost nothing; I have gained a higher quality of life.

3 ■ Get Away from It All

He that can take rest is better than he that can take cities.

—Ben Franklin

Background Even if we get enough sleep and have a rest day each week, we still need longer breaks. The right kind of vacation refreshes us physically, emotionally, and spiritually.

There are two kinds of vacations: the relaxing kind and the *other* kind. Tricia and I like to go places we have never been before, and my business has made it possible for us to travel all over the world. We discovered some years ago that traveling around Europe or Asia for two weeks is not relaxing. That may sound obvious, but we had many disappointing vacations before we figured it out. We still love to do it, but we will take no more than one of these trips every year or two.

I've seen many families take car trips or camping trips or go to someplace like Disneyland, and they invariably come home tired. There's nothing wrong with that kind of vacation if you recognize it for what it is and schedule time to recover before returning to work.

Tricia and I now plan at least one week a year for a truly relaxing vacation. We go to one location and stay there. We choose a place that allows us outdoor recreation—fishing or hiking—but all from a comfortable home base. One of our favorite spots is a friend's cabin on a lake in northern Minnesota.

We've even discovered how to make an overseas trip relaxing. We choose one place, such as a mountain village in Switzerland, and we stay there a whole week, hiking during the day and enjoying the local food at night.

Rejuvenating vacations have helped me make some of the most important decisions in my life. I made my biggest career move after spending a week in a Swiss mountain village. I don't think I could have made the decision any other way. I needed the clarity of being completely alone with my wife, utterly rested, and away from all the pressures of daily living.

Action Take your vacations. If you are someone who feels pride in not taking vacations, you are missing some of the best times of life.

Plan your vacations with the clear understanding of what kind each is to be. Make sure at least one vacation this year is the rejuvenating kind.

If your vacation is likely to leave you tired, come home a few days before you must return to work. Give yourself time to rest, or you're likely to get depressed when you have to go back to work.

Save for vacations. You can't have fun if you're worrying about money. And you don't need to spend a lot to have a good experience. Ask friends for suggestions. One of them just might have a cabin in Minnesota that you can use!

4 ▪▪ Take Miniretreats

To see a world in a grain of sand
And a heaven in a wild flower,
Hold infinity in the palm of your hand
And eternity in an hour.

—William Blake

Background The goal of rest days and vacations is to ultimately bring the peace we feel during our times of rest into our busy times. When I first began working to find more peace in my daily life, the contrast between the times of rest and my daily life was huge. I felt like two different people. No matter how refreshed I was on vacation, the feeling evaporated by 9:00 A.M. on my first day back to work. That is no longer true. I have learned to carry some of it with me all the time.

One way to help you carry a peaceful attitude into your daily routines is to find times for mini-retreats throughout the day.

Action A miniretreat is anything that slows you down, anything that brings enjoyment or gives you perspective.

Find some activities that cause your heart rate to slow just a bit. Set aside times to reflect on what you are doing. Look for the good things in life, and pause to enjoy them.

Have lunch alone occasionally. As a busy executive, I believe this is one of the best things I do for myself. I used to have lunch appointments every day. Almost by accident, I discovered that taking a magazine, leaving the office, and having lunch by myself made my whole day. I was cheerier all afternoon. The time alone brought perspective on the decisions I needed to make or the meetings I had that afternoon. Soon I was refusing to take all but the most important lunch appointments.

You can take a miniretreat almost anywhere. When I'm traveling, I try to avoid my tendency to work or read every minute. Sometimes I'll sit a few minutes and watch people. Sometimes I'll look out the window of the airplane and reflect on my life from the perspective of 32,000 feet.

If you live near mountains, stop what you are doing from time to time and look at them. Go outside tonight and look at the stars, no matter where you live. If you have flowers in your yard, take a moment to stop and smell them. (There's a lot of truth in some clichés!)

Complexity and busyness are like a spiral. The busier we get, the less time we have to pause and reflect. And the less time we pause, the more we take on. We move faster and faster, and we lose the perspective we need to keep our lives focused and simple. Miniretreats are one powerful way to regularly step out of the spiral.

Get Rid of Distractions

A distraction is anything that takes time and doesn't contribute to long-term goals, personal growth, or a peaceful heart. The trouble is, we enjoy many distractions.

5 ∷ Stop the Newspaper

I am sure that I never read any memorable news in a newspaper . . . to a philosopher all news, as it is called, is gossip, and they who edit and read it are old women over their tea. Yet not a few are greedy after this gossip.

—Henry David Thoreau

Background The problem with the newspaper is that it comes first thing every day. It arrives on the doorstep and announces that we must do something with it before we can leave the house. It cries out to be read before the news is no longer news.

Thoreau couldn't understand why people would read the newspaper. He is as right today as he was then: it is primarily gossip, not news. Almost everything in the newspaper is gossip about people, about what *might* happen, or about some tragic events that we'd be just as well off not to know. Thoreau wrote,

If we read of one man robbed, or murdered, or killed by accident, or one house burned, or one vessel wrecked, or one steamboat blown up, or one cow run over on the Western Railroad, or one mad dog killed, or one lot of grasshoppers in the winter,—we never need read of another. One is enough. If you are acquainted with the principle, what do you care for a myriad instances and applications?

I'm not against staying informed. I subscribe to a weekly news magazine. I used to spend several hours a week reading the paper. I can browse through my news magazine in fifteen minutes and know everything I need to know about the world.

There are more words in the Sunday *Los Angeles Times* or *New York Times* than in many books. Ask yourself, How much of real importance do I find in the newspaper?

Action   Cancel your newspaper subscription. If you want to read the paper occasionally, buy it from the newsstand. That will assure it doesn't crowd out more important things. If you buy it only when you have the time and the inclination, you'll soon find you read it far less often.

6 ■■ Turn Off the Television

Amusing Ourselves to Death
—Title of Neil Postman's book about the effects
of TV on our culture

Background You knew this was coming, didn't you? Television is one of the most troubling aspects of our culture. Children today spend thousands of hours watching TV before they even enter school. People in the average household watch seven or eight hours per day. And most of the programming is the entertainment equivalent of junk food.

I grew up on a steady diet of TV. I watched it all —"The Ed Sullivan Show," "Leave It to Beaver," and slightly less classic shows such as "My Mother the Car." I went on into adulthood and graduated to "60 Minutes" and "thirtysomething."

Four years ago, several of our friends decided to cancel their cable TV subscriptions. I was surprised. It was like pulling the life-support system out of the home. Where they live among the mountains, they can't receive any channels without cable.

Tricia and I watched their experiment with interest. Their children fretted mightily at first. But soon they were staying outside and playing with their friends. They were riding their bikes. They had virtually forgotten all about TV within three months. When Christmas came, the children wanted clothes and dolls instead of the latest electronic gadgets. The realization of the effect of advertising on our friends' children convinced Tricia and me to do the same.

At first I was fidgety around the time of my favorite shows. But we began to have exceptional evenings—unlike anything we'd ever experienced. We'd linger over dinner, talking about important topics. We'd listen to our favorite music or read books. We'd hold our young children. As an extra benefit, by canceling our cable subscription, we saved enough money to go out for dinner every other month.

I must admit that we still have a TV, but we only receive two channels. We often rent movies on the weekends, and we watch TV when there is something special like the Olympics. But I am now amazed when I recall how much time I used to waste watching that silly thing. And when I see the promotions for the newest situation comedies, I can hardly believe that sensible adults will waste even a half hour of their lives watching such ridiculous shows. It's like living on Kool-Aid while ignoring life's banquet of experiences.

Action I know that turning off the TV will be difficult for most people in today's culture. I think most of us must go cold turkey. Try it for a week. Agree to watch no TV. See what happens. Don't judge it by the first few days because it's like withdrawing from a drug. If you feel conviction as you read this section, call the cable company before the notion passes. And be prepared to fend off an onslaught from your children.

If abstinence is too much for you, try reviewing what you watch in the upcoming week. Ask your family, "What value did we get from watching this show?"; "Did it teach us something?"; "Did it uplift us, inspire us, or help us in any way?"; "Would we recommend that our friends watch it?"

Over time, cut out those shows that do nothing for you. And avoid leaving the TV on just because you've got nothing better to do. If there's an hour between your favorite shows, turn off the TV and talk or read. See if you can't wean your children and yourselves from spending so much unproductive time in front of the TV.

There's more to life than watching someone else's made-up experiences. Embark on your own real adventures instead.

7 ▚ Limit Magazines, and Read Great Books Instead

How many a man has dated a new era in his life from the reading of a book.
—Henry David Thoreau

Background Like the newspaper, magazines can be intrusive. We know that if we don't read this week's news magazine or this month's food magazine, another one will soon be upon us. We end up reading a magazine before tackling a much more important task because the magazine is dated. I've found myself attacking a stack of magazines just to get through them when I'd really rather be doing something else.

I can think of perhaps two or three memorable magazine articles I've read in my entire life. I tore those articles from the magazines and still have them today. The other five or six hundred articles I've read are now in a landfill somewhere.

My shelves, in contrast, are full of books that have affected my life. *Anna Karenina* awakened me to the deceitfulness of the human heart and vividly portrayed the destructive effects of an extramarital affair. I cannot see a poor person without feeling the sympathy that Dominique La-Pierre's *City of Joy* evoked for a poor Indian rickshaw driver. And as you may have guessed,

Thoreau's *Walden* has had such a profound influence on me that I have nearly worn out my first copy. How much time have I wasted plowing through stacks of magazines while I've virtually ignored the great classics of world literature at the local library?

Action If you subscribe to more magazines than you can comfortably keep up with, stop some of them. If you like to read, read books, especially classics. If a book has been around some time and is famous, there's usually a good reason for it—it has influenced many people.

One caution is still in order. Books can complicate your life, too. If you're the kind of person who has several books going at once, try reading only one at a time.

8 ■■ Stop the Noise

*There can be no very black melancholy to him who
lives in the midst of Nature and has his senses still.*
—Henry David Thoreau

Background Few places left on earth are not
polluted by human-made noise. Tricia and I recently took a backpacking trip through Yosemite.
In very remote wilderness, we were dismayed to
discover that a jet flew overhead every twenty minutes, day and night. We have been in remote areas
of Africa where there is truly no noise other than
wind and birds. It's almost eerie to a person who
lives in the U.S.

I don't believe that our brains were built to with-
stand so much noise. It's a source of stress—a
background kind of stress that we don't even notice. Worse yet, we contribute to it by unnecessar-
ily surrounding ourselves with noise. We have radios in our cars, radios in our homes, and radios to
strap to us when we aren't near the car or the
house. We turn on the TV and leave it on while
we're in another room.

This noise keeps our minds off the things that
really matter. I discovered some time ago that if I
drove home from work in silence, I processed the
happenings of the day. I thought about what went
well and what didn't. I thought about the motives
behind people's actions. I thought about what I
needed to do the next day. By the time I arrived

home, I was ready to put the day behind me. Tricia noticed the difference in me within a few weeks. She said I seemed less preoccupied in the evenings. I now see that when I listened to the radio all the way home, I never processed the day. Thoughts about work kept popping into my mind all evening.

In the past, people sought quiet solitude in the desert or the mountains, and they didn't have anywhere near the amount of noise that we do! We have lost an appreciation of silence.

Action Stop the noise whenever you can. Try riding in the car with the radio off. Be aware of what comes to your mind, and process those things. Ask yourself why they came to mind: Do I need to analyze a situation? Is there a decision I need to make?

Don't turn on the TV if you aren't watching it.

Find times when you can be alone and sit quietly. I often hike into the mountains alone. I use the time to pray and to reflect on my life and any decisions I face. Even a half hour can be greatly refreshing.

9 ⊞ Experiment with Peace

Sometimes, in a summer morning, having taken my accustomed bath, I sat in my sunny doorway from sunrise till noon, rapt in a revery, amidst the pines and hickories and sumachs, in undisturbed solitude and stillness, while the birds sang around or flitted noiseless through the house, until by the sun falling in at my west window, or the noise of some traveller's wagon on the distant highway, I was reminded of the lapse of time. I grew in those seasons like corn in the night, and they were far better than any work of the hands would have been. They were not time subtracted from my life, but so much over and above my usual allowance.

—Henry David Thoreau

Background In our search for simplicity, we need to run counter to our contemporaries and actually get rid of some things that others are striving for. Until we try being without something—not watching TV, turning off the radio in the car, or doing without a second car—we won't know whether it's good for us or not.

The assumption that more things, more friends, and more activities are good for us is flatly wrong. We all have limited time, and unless we focus that time toward truly important things, we will find ourselves wasting vast quantities of it. Our lives will be so full on the outside that we will be empty on the inside. And the worst part of it is this: the more complex our lives become, the less we are aware of it.

Action Cultivate an awareness of your inner peace. Run small experiments in your life, the goal being to measure the effect of a change on your sense of peace. Try going without some thing or activity. Ask yourself, Do I have more or less peace?

Try changing your schedule and consider what it does for your inner peace. Try doing something in the evening if your mornings are terribly busy.

I found a different way to drive to work. It was a less direct route. It took me five minutes longer. But it improved the quality of my life. It avoided the freeway and its associated headaches. The route took me along the foothills of our local mountains. In the evenings, the sun turns the mountains golden, and I have enjoyed many a beautiful drive home after a hard day's work. In short, I changed my perspective on the drive home from looking only at the commuting time to evaluating how I felt.

I avoided buying a computer until long after all my friends owned one. I finally bought one, and in this case, a complex electronic gadget has simplified my life. Writing with a word processing program and paying my bills with a financial package save me many hours and truly simplify the tasks. Experiment with changes in your life, and evaluate whether peace and simplicity are the outcomes.

10 ■■ Know Where Your Time Goes

Do not squander time, for that is the stuff life is made of.

—Ben Franklin

Background Do you know where your time goes? Probably the oldest management advice is simply to know where your time goes. For decades, management experts have advised busy executives to track their time in fifteen-minute blocks for one or two weeks. The advice is excellent for everyone. Most people are quite surprised to discover how they actually spend their time.

Action For one or two weeks, track your time in fifteen-minute increments. Keep a sheet near you, and update it whenever you happen to remember. Do it at least every few hours, or you're apt to forget what you did earlier that day.

When you've completed the exercise, group your activities into reasonable categories—attending meetings, reading, doing chores, talking with the family, going to church, eating meals, and so on—and add up the time in each category.

Then ask yourself,

- Was that activity worthwhile?
- Did it contribute to my goals?

- Did it help someone else?

- Did I have enough time for rest and reflection?

- Did I invest any time in my personal growth?

- Are there things I did that I should delegate to others?

- Are there blocks of time I wasted?

Knowing *where* you spend your time is the first step toward improving *how* you spend it.

Focus Your Life

What do you want from life?

11 ■ Accept Yourself

To thine own self be true.
—William Shakespeare

Background In all the world, there's only one you. No one has your exact genes or your same experiences. The combination is truly unique.

One of the sad facts of life is that few of us are content with ourselves as we are. We think, *If only I looked like her . . . ; If only I made as much money as he does . . . ; If only I could sing like that . . . ; If only I could get a break like she did . . . ;* and on and on.

Action Accept yourself. Life will never be simple until you do. That doesn't mean you should stop growing or give up trying to change bad habits. It means you should stop trying to be someone you're not. If your parents wanted you to be an opera singer and you can't carry a tune, stop feeling guilty. If you don't have the energy to raise two kids, hold down a job, and write a great novel, stop pushing yourself. The novel can wait until the kids grow up.

For many of us, accepting ourselves is very difficult. We may struggle with deep issues that arise from childhood. We may need to seek professional help. As an adult child of alcoholic parents, I can testify to the value of professional help in uncovering some of the hidden drivers in my life.

Take a few minutes to write a description of yourself. Answer these questions:

- What are my strengths?

- What do others say about me?

- What are my weaknesses? Can I accept these weaknesses?

- What unique experiences have I had? (Even negative ones can be used to help others. My current employer likes to hire people who have had at least one business failure. Humility helps in the consulting business!)

- What would I like to change about myself? Are these things reasonable?

- What circumstances dictate my situation right now (for example, having small children)?

Ask your spouse or a friend to review the list with you. Use this self-description to begin accepting yourself.

12 ■ Know Your Values

*I went to the woods because I wished to
live deliberately, . . . and not, when I
came to die, to discover that I had not
lived. I wanted to live deep and suck out
all the marrow of life.*
—Henry David Thoreau

Background   What is most important to you in
life? Is there anything you'd be willing to die for? Is
there anything you feel passionate about?

The things that mean the very most to us repre-
sent our values. If I'm willing to die to protect my
family, family is obviously a very high value in my
life. If I'm willing to die for my country, patriotism
is a high value.

Similarly, each of us is willing to invest time in
certain things. A friend of mine has two young children and a full-time job. That's enough to keep anyone busy, but he has been going to night school
for two years to earn his law degree. He and his
wife place a high value on education and personal
growth. If they didn't, they'd never be willing to
sacrifice as much as they have to pursue the degree.

We need to clarify our values because our goals
will arise from them. And if we don't keep our values in mind, the myriad demands on our time will
tend to crowd out the things that are most essential. I have another friend who still gets tears in his

eyes every time he tells me about his regrets in neglecting his family. His value system said that family was the most vital thing in his life, yet he allowed his career to keep him away from home most of the time while his children were growing up. That time can never be made up. It's a too-familiar story.

Action List your top five values. Making this list will be a prelude to the next step, identifying your goals.

What things do you hold most dear in life? They might include the following:

- Having a good relationship with God

- Having a solid relationship with your spouse

- Investing in children

- Achieving personal growth

- Developing your gifts

- Attaining financial security

- Cultivating friendships

- Participating in church-related activities

- Giving

- Serving others

- Keeping a simple life

Developing a separate list for work can also be useful. When I made a list for my role as vice president of World Vision, it included caring for each employee, creating an entrepreneurial environment where ideas are freely exchanged, and having a service orientation toward our donors. I posted a list of my five top values near my desk. It reminded me each day to focus on what was most important.

13 ■ Set Clear Goals

Most people vastly overestimate what they can accomplish in a day and vastly underestimate what they can accomplish in five years.

—Ted W. Engstrom

Background Most of us are reluctant to set goals. We think, *If I set a goal, it seems that I'm setting myself up to fail. I'm putting pressure on myself, and there's a good chance I'll be disappointed.*

I thought that way until a few years ago. I had so many things going on in my life that I finally faced the fact I couldn't do all of them. I was trying to write three books, consult with two companies, and continue my full-time job. I knew I had to prioritize.

I started by reflecting on my values. I then sorted through all my projects and set three simple goals for the rest of that year. I was amazed at the sense of clarity the exercise gave me. I've been hooked on setting goals ever since.

Goals help us say no. When our goals are clear, we avoid the tendency to take on more than we can actually do. We also can avoid the many distractions in our lives—the little things that seem important at the moment but really have little value, such as reading the newspaper. And people get far more done when they focus on completing just a few things rather than run from task to task with priorities constantly reshuffling.

Action   Set three goals for yourself for the next two years. If you could accomplish only three things in the next two years, what would they be?

Now back up and set three goals for the next ninety days. What three things can you do in the next ninety days to make significant progress toward your two-year goals?

With these ninety-day goals in mind, what three things should you do this week?

With a little practice, you'll find that you can use this simple goal-setting exercise for all the areas of your life. I have goals for my personal life, my professional life, my weight, my finances, and so on.

I have learned that the best times for me to set goals are the beginning of the new year and my birthday. These are times when I naturally look forward. I review my goals about once a month.

Don't be afraid to fall short of your goals. My experience is that I achieve about two-thirds of my goals. Some goals will change due to circumstances; some will change because you changed your mind. That's all right. Goals are not to be shackles but to be tools to bring focus to your life today. Be flexible with them.

14 ∷ Learn to Say No

We are much more apt to ask, "How can we do it?" than "What's worthwhile doing?"

—Sam Keen

Background   *No* is one of the hardest words I know to say. Those of us who love people and want to be loved are reluctant to turn others down. There have been many times when I felt I should stay home to be with my family. Instead, I've found myself agreeing to do something someone asked me to do.

Saying no is much easier if you have clear goals. If you know you have a problem with taking on too much, and you haven't set clear goals, go back to the last chapter, and do yourself a big favor by setting them.

I've been helped by realizing that even Jesus couldn't do everything. He came to one small corner of the world, and on a given day He touched only a few people. Even then He often withdrew to the mountains to be alone. He knew He needed times of prayer and rest. He had a core group of twelve disciples because He knew He couldn't invest Himself adequately in more. Among the Twelve, three were his closest friends, and one was called "the disciple whom Jesus loved."

If Jesus knew His limitations, surely we can admit that we have some, too.

Action Practice saying no. If something arises that is not consistent with your current goals, refuse to get involved. Nothing saves time faster than refusing to get involved in the first place. If it is pressing, and you feel perhaps you should do it, revise your goals and drop something else.

Protect time to be with your family. It's perfectly legitimate to tell someone, "I'm sorry, but we already have plans that night." Your plans could be to stay home as a family.

Say no to the phone. Tricia and I will not interrupt a nice dinner to answer the phone. We have an answering machine, and if a friend calls, we'll return the call later that night. The phone does not give others the right to interrupt you at their convenience!

15 ■■ Plan Ahead

Diligence is the mother of good fortune.
—Miguel de Cervantes

Background A wealthy industrialist once asked a management consultant to follow him through the day and advise him on how to be more effective. At the end of the day, the consultant presented a simple idea: "Before you go home each night, make a list of what you hope to get done the next day. Then prioritize the list. When you come in the next day, start working on number one. Don't go on to number two until number one is done. Do the same with each item." The industrialist asked for the consultant's bill, but the consultant told him to try the idea for two weeks and then pay him whatever he thought it was worth. Three weeks later, the consultant received a check for $25,000, a huge sum in those days.

Action This is one of the simplest and most effective time management techniques ever invented. If you follow it, you'll never fall behind on the things that really matter.

Late each day, list the priorities for the next day. Part of the genius in this idea is that your perspective on the next day is clear and unhurried at the end of the previous day.

Cultivate Your Spirit

You are a three-part creature—body, soul, and spirit. The spirit has been greatly neglected in modern life.

16 ■ Start Every Day with God

In all your ways acknowledge [God],
And He shall direct your paths.
—Proverbs 3:6

Background The soul is the locus of the personality, emotions, and will. The spirit is a higher part of the individual. It's the part with a conscience. It can sense God and communicate with Him. It speaks to us from time to time about deep values that should be guiding our lives. It reminds us of obligations.

Self-help groups such as Alcoholics Anonymous (AA) have found that recovery is much more likely if the person nurtures the spiritual side. For instance, AA talks of a relationship with a "higher power." They have found that alcoholics recover better when they define for themselves some higher power and ask that higher power for help. Psychologist John Bradshaw tells the tongue-in-cheek story of a young man who chose a tree as his higher power. One day he ran into his group meeting in a panic. The other members tried to get him to calm down. Finally, he said, "They cut down my higher power!"

For me, that higher power is Jesus Christ. Having been raised without a firm foundation in any faith, I know what a difference Jesus Christ can make. Tricia and I drifted in our early adulthood, ending up involved in drugs. When we opened our lives to the God of the Bible and asked forgiveness through Jesus Christ, we truly began to live. We turned our lives over to Him, and He has done wonderful things in us as we yield to Him and His will each day to the best of our ability. I would not live one more day without Christ for all the riches in the world.

Action   Start every day with at least a few minutes focusing on God. If you can, set aside a half hour to read devotional material, reflect on it, and pray. If you can take more time, that's all the better. If you can't afford that much time right now, do whatever you can. At a minimum, pray a few minutes.

There's nothing better than time with God to focus your day. It's a pause that reminds you that you aren't alone. Someone will help and guide you. The busier your day, the more you need a few minutes of quiet preparation.

17 ■ Practice Awareness of God

The time of business does not with me differ from the time of prayer; and in the noise and clatter of my kitchen, while several persons are at the same time calling for different things, I possess God in as great tranquillity as if I were upon my knees at the blessed sacrament.

—Brother Lawrence

Background This monk, Brother Lawrence, has inspired millions to cultivate an awareness of God since he wrote his seventeenth-century classic book *The Practice of the Presence of God.* His one point is that anyone can sense God's presence virtually all the time.

God is always here. We forget Him, not the other way around. We can learn to remember Him throughout our day, and this awareness will bring clarity, peace, and simplicity to our lives.

Action The practice of awareness of God's presence is simple. Seek to remember Him as often as possible. Allow things in your life to remind you of Him—the beauty of flowers and trees, the song of a bird, whatever works.

Whenever you remember God, pray silently, thanking Him that He is still with you, asking Him to guide you, asking Him to keep reminding you that He is with you.

Practicing awareness of God doesn't happen easily. Many people have worked at it for weeks or months and still feel they are only just beginning. If you get discouraged, remember that even the desire is a sign that you're well on your way.

18 ∷ Turn Off the Adrenaline

Don't hurry, don't worry. You're only here for a short visit.

—Walter C. Hagen

Background   Our bodies give us one very simple and accurate clue to whether we are living peacefully—it's adrenaline. Adrenaline production was intended as a survival mechanism. For short periods of time, it allows the body to perform far beyond normal capabilities. It boosts heart rate, dilates blood vessels, heightens awareness, pulls blood away from the extremities toward vital organs, increases muscular strength, and deadens pain.

Due to the effects of adrenaline, human beings have lifted cars to free persons pinned underneath; soldiers have run or dragged themselves when their wounds were nearly fatal. And athletes perform at their peak ability by psyching themselves into producing adrenaline.

There's a dark side to adrenaline. The body pays a price for it. People have performed superhuman feats, completely unaware that they were tearing muscles in the process. But an even bigger problem is that many of us are pumping adrenaline through our systems nearly every day. The body was not intended to endure so much.

Some doctors now believe that adrenaline may be the link between Type A behavior and heart disease. Type A behavior is largely a modern phenomenon. Persons with Type A behavior are driven to accomplishments. They find it difficult to rest or to wait. They are always hurrying. I believe we are not born this way; our modern culture works with our own anxieties and produces adrenaline.

Many of us are often aware of our cold hands—the surest sign of adrenaline flowing. Others develop headaches, tightness in the neck and shoulders, or perspiration.

We must turn off the adrenaline. It's appropriate when we are truly in a fight-or-flight situation (for example, facing a mugger), when we are working toward a peak performance (for example, preparing for a public speech or an athletic event), or when an emergency calls for all our strength. It's not appropriate when we are driving in traffic, discussing a pet project with a colleague, or interacting with our families.

Action   The first step is to become aware of adrenaline. The cold hands are the easiest sign to spot. Begin to be aware when adrenaline starts to surge through your system.

The second step is to be reflective immediately. When you're aware of adrenaline, ask yourself, Is it appropriate? Do I need the adrenaline to handle this situation, or am I overreacting?

The third step is to take positive steps to cool down. I have learned that if I am upset in traffic and developing that familiar urge to dart around the slow cars, I should pick one lane and stay in it. If I'm getting off the freeway in a few miles, I'll stay in the right lane. If I'm going a long way, I'll pick one of the middle lanes and stay there. Once I make the decision, it's surprising how quickly I calm down.

Stopping the adrenaline will take practice. If I'm upset in a business meeting, I may not have the opportunity to excuse myself and take a leisurely walk to the water cooler. But I can at least be aware of my adrenaline and try my best to keep perspective on the meeting. Rarely is it a matter of life-and-death consequences.

When you're not able to avoid a burst of adrenaline, you should schedule time to recover. Your body was not meant to sustain that pace, and you need to give it a break. After a speech, I'll try to leave time to sleep late the next morning. After a tough morning of meetings, I'll have lunch by myself. The most critical issue is to not allow the fast pace to carry on any longer than necessary. As soon as possible, slow down.

19 ■ Advance with a Retreat

I love to be alone. I never found the companion that was so companionable as solitude.

—Henry David Thoreau

Background When we think of taking a retreat, we usually don't think of the literal meaning of the word: to move backward. In reality, taking a personal retreat is a big move forward. Perhaps we should call it an advance.

Have you ever taken one whole day just to be alone? I'd never done such a thing until a few years ago. I had to be in another town, and I had most of the day alone. At the time, I didn't like being alone. It made me nervous. I felt lonely.

For some reason, at that particular time of my life, I felt I had some personal work to do. I was dissatisfied and didn't know why. I knew I'd never figure it out until I could spend time alone.

I took a notebook and began by working through the high points of the last few years: What was I most happy with? Then I worked through the low points: What would I like to change? When I began feeling restless, I'd change scenery—go to a mall or drive to the beach. For seven or eight hours, I wrestled with myself. Some of the most fundamental directions in my life today are the result of that time. I resolved to get in shape. I resolved to explore the effects of my troubled childhood with a counselor. I resolved to show more love to my wife and to give work a smaller place in my heart so there would be more room for her.

Since that time, I've tried to repeat this experience at least twice a year.

Action   Schedule time to take a retreat. If you're a businessperson, perhaps you can take an earlier flight when you have to travel and use the time in another city. If you're a parent, hire a baby-sitter and find a quiet place in the library or at a park.

Many churches will help with retreats. The older traditions—Catholic, Lutheran, Episcopalian —tend to actively promote this idea for their members. They often have their own retreat centers, which are usually available to anyone.

Start your retreat with prayer. Prayer opens your spirit to God's influence. If you aren't practiced with prayer, don't worry. It's the heart that matters, not the eloquence.

Reflect on the past. Where have you fallen short? What are you most happy with?

Consider the future. What would you like to change? Be sure to write—the more, the better. You will be surprised at the passion that flows, and if you don't write it down, you'll forget important elements of your thought process.

Close your retreat with prayer. Offer your plans and dreams to God, and ask Him to give you the strength to carry out your good intentions.

Make Peace with Your Enemies

Life is too short to spend it in hate. Hate consumes the hater more than the hated.

20 ■ Forgive

To err is human, to forgive divine.
—Alexander Pope

Background Unforgiveness can ruin your life. When someone slights you, offends you, or deeply hurts you, the urge to respond in kind is a natural reaction: an eye for an eye, a tooth for a tooth. But giving in to that urge takes its toll not only on the offender; it can consume the one seeking revenge.

In biblical times, Jewish law allowed for such revenge. Whatever someone did to you, you were allowed to do to that person. If you were killed, your relatives could take the life of your killer. To prevent hasty "justice" when someone may have been killed by accident, the law established cities of refuge. If you killed someone accidentally, you could flee to a city of refuge, and as long as you remained within that city, no one could touch you. If you ever ventured outside the city, you could be killed. Some relatives would wait for years to catch a man outside the city and kill him in revenge.

The Hatfields and the McCoys were real people. Their feud entered into legend and stretched across several generations. Today, various ethnic groups in the Middle East, Catholics and Protestants in Northern Ireland, and gangs in East Los Angeles perpetuate revenge that is out of control.

Far more common are the little things that we

let separate us from family members and friends. Someone said something and we let it fester for years. An argument that developed on one of our bad days blew up into a lifelong break with a brother. A friend lets us down and we stop investing in that friendship.

Action The nature of human beings is such that we grate on one another at times. It happens in the best of relationships. We must learn to forgive. Forgiveness means that I choose to let you be imperfect. I accept you even though you may have hurt me.

Being forgiving doesn't mean just rolling over and accepting the situation. If someone offends you, you should go to that person and say what's bothering you. The hurt gets out into the open where it can be dealt with. If the person refuses to apologize, you should ask someone else to be an arbitrator. The third party can help you and the person be fair to each other.

Ultimately, if the person apologizes, you have no choice but to forgive. If the person won't apologize, you have a tough choice. Will you let this situation separate you permanently from the other person, or will you find it in yourself to forgive anyway? Unless the offense really does deserve to separate the two of you (for example, repeated unfaithfulness of a spouse), you will be far better off if you can find the strength to forgive.

Sometimes people hurt you deeply, especially if it's someone you love very much. Offering forgiveness doesn't mean the pain will stop. Rather, each time the pain comes back, you look beyond it. I like to think in terms of driving on a dark road at night. When the oncoming headlights are in your eyes, you can steer by the white line at the side of the road. When the hurt returns, you remember that you have made a choice to forgive, and you do your best to look away from the hurt and to continue moving forward.

21 ■ Channel Your Anger

Anger is the emotion that tells us our boundaries are being violated.
—John Bradshaw

Background Having enemies takes enormous energy. When I have an enemy, I must stay on guard. I must watch my flank lest my enemy take advantage of me. I imagine all sorts of conversations with my enemy—how I'd like to tell him a thing or two! These imaginary conversations can consume all my waking thoughts.

I have had to work diligently at dealing with enemies in my life. It's hard for me to confront another person when I feel my rights are violated. I'd rather suffer in silence, just suck it in.

I saw a cartoon recently that made me laugh out loud. It showed a series of caves with cavemen standing out front. All the cavemen were looking in the direction of one particular cave. In front of that cave was a portly caveman; he was sloppily dressed and surrounded by mastodon bones and carcasses. The caption read, "There's one in every neighborhood."

We lived in a neighborhood that had its own version of this caveman—the guy with a boat, an RV, and four cars. His vehicles lined the street in front of my house for months. I'd smile at the man, but inwardly, I was seething. I began to imagine that he left the vehicles there to make me mad. I pictured going down to his house to ask him to move the vehicles, but in my imagination he always said something nasty, which would cause me to respond in kind. I decided a confrontation wasn't worth it, and I tried to ignore the situation.

Finally, the day came when we put our house up for sale. Our agent suggested that we should clear the street in front of our house, or its value might be diminished. I was forced to act. I gritted my teeth, marched down to the neighbor, and steeled myself for the scene to come. What happened was what I had least expected. My neighbor said he'd be glad to move them, and they were never again in front of my house.

The point is, not until we take positive steps to resolve anger will we be able to have peace.

Forgiving my neighbor in advance would have softened my anger. I could have asked him to move his vehicles without fear of exploding at him. I could have decided that if he wouldn't move them, it wouldn't mean he was an awful person. If I had to, I could live with the situation. I'd rather look at the vehicles than hate a neighbor.

At our next house, we found we could see a neighbor's old boat until the trees leaved out in the spring. Soon after meeting him, I asked my neighbor if he'd move the boat in the fall. He agreed without hesitation.

Anger is actually a healthy emotion. It creates problems when we don't act appropriately on it.

Action   When you feel anger, act on it that very day. If you do, there's much less chance of its getting out of control. Repressed anger will someday burst forth like a volcano.

Tricia and I have a compact that if we are even slightly offended by each other, we will bring it up the same day. If I cut her off while talking to friends, she'll let me know later that night that I hurt her feelings. Before our agreement, I would have found out about the offense months later, after I'd done it a dozen times. By then, it would have come out in an explosion, "You always cut me off, and I'm sick of it . . ." I would then, of course, respond defensively. Now, we rarely have angry arguments. We are able to deal with the normal tensions of married life productively.

Resolve to act quickly and positively when you feel anger, before it grows into something out of proportion to the problem. Don't become a Hatfield or a McCoy.

22 ■■ Seek Help for Difficult Relationships

Fifty percent of married couples will probably never be happy unless they get genuine professional help.
—David Olson, University of Minnesota researcher, from a study of 15,300 couples

Background Sometimes a relationship is just not working. You seem to be spiraling downward. If the relationship is important, it's worth seeking help. These days many professionals can help you work through relationship problems. And many of these problems stem from past experiences, often in your childhood. Trying to work through them on your own is not nearly as effective as gaining insights from an unbiased, well-qualified outsider.

I've seen many marriages, including my own, where the two people are driven by needs they don't understand, needs arising from childhood. The needs of one can feed right into the needs of the other and create a seemingly impossible situation.

I have two friends, a man and a woman, who seem made for each other. All their friends want them to get married. But they have been on-again, off-again for six years now. He has a fear of abandonment, stretching back to his childhood. He needs a woman who will be committed to him. Because she has been unable to make this commitment, he is now paralyzed by fear, an irrational fear that, even if they marry, she will ultimately leave him.

She, in turn, has a fear of conditional love since she never felt that she was intrinsically worthy of love. Love was always given to her based on her performance. She needs a man who will not pressure her to get married because she feels she is loved only as long as she performs. Pressure to marry feels to her like conditional love. They are seeking professional help, and the outcome is not yet clear. But at least they are doing something positive about the difficult relationship.

Action   If you are having serious difficulties in a close relationship, life will not seem simple until you deal with the root problems. No matter what else you do to simplify your life, the relationship will weigh on you. Seek help.

There are lots of alternatives these days: marriage and family counselors, psychologists, and psychiatrists. These professionals specialize in relational problems and must undergo certification in most states, assuring that they've had proper education and internship.

Many churches offer free counseling by a pastor trained in counseling.

One word of caution is in order: Be sure the counselor shares your values. You'll want to determine this at the beginning. I've heard sad tales of counselors who drove wedges in marriages by their biases. One woman I know was advised to leave her husband because "women are better off alone, free of the restrictions of a marriage." I know another woman whose counselor made inappropriate sexual comments to her. Fortunately, she saw this early and got out before she became vulnerable.

Simplify Your Finances

Control your money; don't let it control you.

23 ■ Use a Budget

Instead of studying how to make it worth men's while to buy my baskets, I studied rather how to avoid the necessity of selling them.

—Henry David Thoreau

Background Thoreau's wisdom on this point is profound and rarely followed. For all the energy we put into trying to get more money, we might put just a little into reducing our need for money instead!

You cannot have simplicity in your finances without a budget. You cannot have control over your money unless you know where it's going and make decisions about it *in advance.* Unfortunately, thousands of individuals and companies out there want your money. And they aren't shy about going after it. Marketers study what makes you tick and how to get you to part with your money for things you don't really need.

A major marketing study a few years ago discovered that the deepest felt need for men in America was companionship. For women, the deepest need was to be cherished. Notice the most common theme in commercials? For products aimed at men, it's a group of buddies having fun together. For products aimed at women, it's being caressed because your skin is so soft or kissed because your mouth is so fresh and so on.

There are a thousand other tricks in the marketer's hat. Believe me; I've been one for over ten years. Studies have been done on everything from the layout of the store to the type of music played —all designed to make you spend more money.

The only way you can navigate the treacherous waters of the Buy Me Sea and safely reach the other side is to make wise decisions about money away from the point of purchase. That's exactly what a budget does. You make your decisions in advance, and you track your expenses against those decisions, making course corrections as necessary.

Action   If you've never done a budget, don't be intimidated. A budget doesn't have to be so restrictive that it takes all the fun out of life. Tricia and I have found it to be freeing. We even give ourselves an allowance—a little money each month that we can spend however we desire.

To prepare a budget, do the best you can to reconstruct where your money went last month. Take your checkbook, pay stubs, and charge account statements, and combine expenses into ten or fifteen categories—for example, auto, clothing, food, housing, and entertainment. If you pay many of your expenses in cash, you may not be able to reconstruct all of last month. You may need to keep track for a month or two. If it's too tedious to write down every expense for a month, note how much cash you have available for each day and endeavor at the end of the day to identify where it went.

When you have some history, develop a rough

plan for where you want to spend your money this month. Track it as closely as you can, and evaluate at the end of the month how well you did. With some experience, you'll find you are making changes. You'll decide to cut back a little in one area to avoid going into debt or to save for a major purchase.

The hardest part of budgeting is that you may find that you are spending more than you are making. Although that's a rude awakening, it's better to know it now than to figure it out when you're nearly bankrupt!

If you have a computer, several programs are available (for example, Quicken and Managing Your Money) that will reduce the amount of time it takes to pay bills and balance the checkbook. And they automatically keep track of actual expenses versus a budget. Using a computerized approach has been a great help to Tricia and me. We take at most a half hour each month to review the report that Quicken prints out for us and discuss changes to the budget for the next month.

24 ■■ Pay Off Your Mortgage Early

Thirty-year mortgages make mortgage companies rich.

—Charles J. Givens

Background If you borrowed $100,000 at 10 percent interest for thirty years, after ten years of making payments you would have paid the mortgage company $105,000—more than you originally owed—and you would still owe $91,000. That is not a misprint. The fact is, when you spread payments over thirty years, you are paying virtually nothing toward the principal on your loan until the last ten years. And if you ever reach that glorious day when you have made the last payment, be aware that you have paid a total of $316,000—more than three times what you borrowed.

If you added only $200 per month to your payment to be used against principal, you would have paid $129,000 in ten years, but you would owe only $50,000. Your mortgage would be paid off in fifteen years, at a total cost of $193,000. By adding only $200 per month, you save $123,000 in interest. And what will you do with all the money you have for the next fifteen years, free of mortgage payments?

Less than 2 percent of Americans own their homes free and clear. The majority of retirees still carry a mortgage that has more years remaining than their projected life span. By paying only $200 more a month (or proportionally more if you owe more than $100,000), you can own your home in fifteen years and save $100,000 or more in interest.

Action Start this month. Find the money somewhere. Pay an extra $200 per month toward your mortgage, and determine to own your home while you're still young enough to enjoy the freedom. Can you imagine how much you will simplify your life when you no longer have a mortgage payment? Keep asking yourself that question and you will soon not miss the $200.

The only qualification to this advice is that some mortgages contain a prepayment penalty. They are rare these days, but ask your lender to be sure that your loan agreement allows you to prepay toward the principal.

25 ■■ Fast from Buying

Background We all have our soft spots. For me, it tends to be books. For my wife, it's clothes. Both of us have a weakness for going out to eat.

It's important that we break these spending habits from time to time, especially if we have a tendency to buy things to lift our spirits when we're feeling blue, or if we tend to buy on impulse.

A fast from buying is simply a decision that I won't buy something for a specified period of time. I might decide that I have enough unread books to last awhile. No matter how many great books I see, I will not buy another one until I finish the ones I have. Tricia will occasionally decide not to buy any clothes for a few months. We may decide not to eat out this month because we are adjusting our budget to save for a large purchase.

Far from stifling, these fasts are freeing. One decision can save dozens of smaller ones. I can learn to be more detached from what I own. I can focus on lifting my spirits by enjoying nature or seeking a closer relationship with God rather than making a trip to the mall.

Action If anything is getting the best of your budget, decide to go on a fast. Determine that no matter what happens, you will not spend money on that particular item for a specified period of time. It's much easier to accumulate useless things than it is to live wisely. To live simply in our consumer culture, we must live above the seduction that is constantly trying to get us to define ourselves by what we own. We must not buy what we do not need. If we hope to live up to that commitment, we must occasionally fast from buying even good things. It's good for building discipline.

26 ■■ Save 10 Percent for Yourself

And you shall spend that money for whatever your heart desires: for oxen or sheep, for wine or similar drink, for whatever your heart desires; you shall eat there before the LORD your God, and you shall rejoice, you and your household.
—Deuteronomy 14:26

Background   Who says God is no fun? God set a practice here that amounts to a giant party.

Life has enough trials without constant financial worries. As I have progressed in my business career, I have learned one certain truth: I'll never have *enough* money. No matter how big the raises, they always disappear into my budget.

The only solution to this dilemma is to budget ourselves to live on 90 percent of our income. Personally, I try to make do with 80 percent, so I can give away 10 percent and save another 10 percent.

If you can save 10 percent of your income, it's amazing what happens to your attitude. There's always a cushion. There's no more fear when the car breaks down, the tax bill is higher than expected, or an appliance needs to be replaced. Charles J. Givens, in his book *Wealth Without Risk,* suggests you save at this level for two years until you have 20 percent of your annual income in savings. He calls it "attitude money."

Action It's not pleasant to think of saving money for two years just to have a cushion, but it's one of the soundest pieces of advice I've seen. Develop a budget and work toward saving 10 percent each month. In chapter 31, "Invest Simply," I'll tell you what to do with the money.

After you've saved two years' worth—when you have 20 percent of your annual income in savings —start spending that 10 percent each year on whatever your heart desires, as the Bible suggests. Life will seem a lot more pleasant.

27 ■ Have Fun Saving Money

I like ironing your shirts now that I get paid for it!

—My wife, Tricia

Background No one likes to save money, right? Wrong. You can make saving money fun. The secret is to come up with creative ways to reward yourself for saving.

Tricia has always hated ironing, so I've done my own shirts. When I began traveling frequently, I no longer had the time. I decided to start taking my shirts to the cleaners. Then I had an idea. If Tricia ironed any of my shirts, I'd give her the same amount of money that I'd pay the cleaners. It would be "above-budget" money. In other words, if she had spent the budgeted amount for clothes already, she could use this extra money she earned from ironing. Much to my surprise, she began to enjoy ironing! She also saves coupons now —something she had never wanted to do. She keeps track of how much she saves, and she uses the money for whatever she wants. We already give ourselves a monthly allowance to spend on whatever we wish. This extra money is over and above that.

A friend takes his wife to Florida every year on

what they save using coupons. Another friend goes to Europe on the money he and his wife save from having only one car. He takes the train to work every day—an inconvenience, certainly—but the payoff is worth it. They love their yearly vacation in Europe.

Action Think of ways you could save money, but you haven't been motivated enough to do it—clipping coupons, taking your lunch to work, making do with one car, taking a cheaper flight, and so on. Then think of a way to reward the family member who made the sacrifice, or decide to share the reward—have a night out for dinner, a vacation, or something that the whole family will enjoy.

28 ■■ Avoid Debt

Debt is the worst poverty.
—M. G. Lightner

Background Debt is one sure way to complicate life. The more debt you have, the less control you have over your finances, and the more your energy and thoughts will be consumed with money. You have to work harder just to stay even.

We live in a society that encourages debt for virtually any expense. Only a few decades ago, even home mortgages were given for ten years or less, and it was impossible to get loans for cars. These days people use charge cards for virtually anything, even groceries.

Action Avoid debt. Don't borrow to buy anything unless you could resell what you bought and pay off the loan (such as a house or a stable investment). Even for a house, use the strategy discussed in chapter 24 to pay off the mortgage in fifteen years, saving $100,000 or more in interest.

If you cannot discipline yourself to pay off your charge cards every month, cut them up. Never go into debt for things like clothes, vacations, or stereo equipment. If you have trouble paying the money back, you have nothing to sell. You are a slave to that debt.

Buying a new car on credit is poor stewardship

of your resources. If you borrow money to buy a new car, it will be two years before you owe less than what the car is worth. In other words, if you have to sell the car, you will need to come up with extra money to pay off the loan. Let others take this huge loss. If you need a car, buy one that's two years old. It's still relatively new, but it's past the time when a car's value drops rapidly.

Most banks will loan on two-year-old cars at close to the same interest rate as new cars. (They know that a two-year-old car is a good value!)

29 ■ Ignore Fads and Fashions

Hang the fashions. Buy only what you need.

—Richard Foster

Background Fashions are an incredible waste of money. A coat is discarded because it's out-of-date, even though it still performs its function perfectly well. A closet is full of ties too wide or too narrow. Practically new pants are the "wrong" color.

Fashions are created by the clothing industry. Some smart person long ago figured out that fashion trends could induce people to buy far more clothes than they really need.

You don't have to give in to this pressure.

Action Refuse to buy trendy clothes. You know when something is likely to be a short-lived fashion.

Men can avoid the problem with suits and ties by loading up when the lapel and tie widths are somewhere in the middle. Don't buy when they're at their widest or narrowest. If you really feel you need to look up-to-date, buy just one of the latest wild ties. Resist the temptation to look trendy every day.

It's a little more difficult for women, but there are skirt lengths and classic cuts that never go out of style.

Abiding by this suggestion is more difficult with children. Their self-images are fragile, and the peer pressure is intense. Don't be so strict that they suffer constant embarrassment, but do set limits. Some of the trends, such as superexpensive tennis shoes, are ridiculous.

For every season and every occasion, there are some clothes that are always in style. Fill most of your wardrobe with them, and wear them until they're worn out.

Keep your children away from TV, and they won't be clamoring for the latest toy. I think it's a crime to let children spend endless hours playing with electronic gadgets when there's a whole world for them to experience and explore. Buy them toys that stretch their minds, for example, telescopes or microscopes; better yet, take them out into the great outdoors, and teach them about the local plants and animals.

If we could escape from the bombardment of advertising, we'd soon realize we need very little to live a full life. Unfortunately, we can't get away from it, but we can fight against the temptation to have the latest, greatest new thing.

30 ❖ Don't Compete with the Joneses

There are two ways to get enough: one is to continue to accumulate more and more. The other is to desire less.
—G. K. Chesterton

Background Keeping up with the Joneses is an age-old game. If we don't look as prosperous as the folks next door, how can we hold our heads high in the neighborhood? There's no end to this game—and no winner.

Action Impress people with your life, not with your things. And don't let your children use their friends as the standard for what they need. Teach them while they're young that the only standard we live by is what is right for us. We develop our standards by being sensitive to God and neighbor but never by trying to keep up with the neighbor.

Buy items such as cars and clothes for function, not for the potential to impress others.

31 ■■ Invest Simply

There are two times in a man's life when he should not speculate: when he can't afford it, and when he can.

—Mark Twain

Background Investments can complicate our lives in one of two ways. First, we can be so driven to get the highest return possible that we take unwise risks and end up losing money. Almost everyone I know has lost some money this way. Fortunately, it's been a lesson we've learned before we had much money to invest. There's an old adage among investment professionals that says, "If it sounds too good to be true, it is."

The other way is to let investments worry us. If we are worrying about our money, we may as well give it away. Life is too short to spend it worrying about money. I've never seen a rich person I thought was happy because of the money. And I've seen Ethiopians with nothing who were joyful and happy.

I'm not going to say, "Get rid of your money." For most of us, investments are necessary—to provide for our children's education and our old age if nothing else.

Simple investments are within our reach. Simple investments have a track record of reasonable returns through all types of economic ups and downs. They are secure—they can't be easily stolen or evaporate when a risky deal goes sour.

And they are places we can leave our money without needing to make decisions week by week or even month by month.

Action   One simple investment is the stock market—but not individual stocks. You should never buy individual stocks unless you are a professional. Forget all the hot tips; all the decks are stacked against the individual investor. If your Uncle Harry knows something about a company, the pros knew it long ago, and it's already reflected in the price. That is, unless Uncle Harry works for the company and is giving you inside information. In that case, you and Harry can go to jail if you profit from it.

Stock mutual funds are probably the best long-term investment for individuals. They return approximately 12 percent per year over the long haul. They are, however, subject to many ups and downs along the way, and you should not invest money in stock mutual funds that you may need to pull out on short notice. You should also not invest a lump sum all at once. The market may go down next week and you are suddenly behind. Do what the pros call dollar cost-averaging. Invest a little at a time, every week or every month. Over time, your price per share will average out, and you stand a better chance of making a good return.

Money market funds provide a safe alternative for money that you may need soon. They return less than stocks, but they are much less subject to fluctuation. They usually allow you to write checks against your account.

Rental houses have also tended to be a good investment for the average individual investor. The main problem with rental houses is that you have the headaches of maintaining the homes, dealing with tenants, advertising, and so on. The tax laws are hard to keep up with, too. I don't think rental houses will simplify your life, but if you have time —if you are retired, for example—they can be good investments.

Invest simply, and give up trying to make a killing.

32 ◼◼ Give It Away

As the purse is emptied, the heart is filled.
—Victor Hugo

Background Are you tired of money controlling you? Jacques Ellul, in his book *Money and Power,* uses Jesus' teachings about money to make the case that money is a rival god. It tends to take over your life. You serve and worship it without even realizing it. He prescribes the way to break that rival god's hold on your life: when you give money away, you profane it. You step outside its rules, which include: hoard and you'll have more, have more and you'll be happier, and so on. When you give, you prove to yourself again and again that money is not the root of happiness.

Your money will always have an unnatural hold on you until you learn to give. No matter what your financial status, there are always others worse off. If you earn the median income in the United States, you are included in the top 5 percent of the wealthiest people who have ever lived. Believe me, I've been all over the world, and we have it far better than we care to admit.

I believe as citizens of one globe we owe it to help others, especially the poor in other countries. I don't know how to bring equity to the situation, but as World Vision's founder Bob Pierce said,

"Just because you can't do everything doesn't mean you can't do something."

As a Christian, I believe my giving should be significant. It's not enough to give only a few dollars here and there. I use the guideline that God gave to the Jewish people in the Old Testament, 10 percent. Tricia and I give away at least 10 percent of our gross income each month, as though it were another bill to pay. That's the minimum. We try to see how far we can exceed that level. We consider it an obligation as children of God and citizens of a needy world.

Action   Begin this month to give. If your budget is tight, give what you can. But change your budget so you can give more.

Find one or two charities that focus on causes you care deeply about. Read their literature. Become informed about the causes. Request the charities' annual reports, and pay close attention to the percentage spent on fund-raising and administration. Anything over 25 or 30 percent is unreasonable.

Most charities are listed with the Better Business Bureau (BBB). If the charity is not approved by the BBB, find another one.

Don't just give to causes far away; give locally, too. If you go to church, give to the church. If you are benefiting from the pastor and the programs, contribute to their support.

You will be especially rewarded if you can give to something locally and see the rewards of your giving. Visit a local shelter or soup kitchen and watch your gifts at work.

I also believe in direct giving to the homeless in my community. They are reminders of how blessed I am. I don't want to always cross the street to avoid them. I want to say some kind words, learn more about their situation, and do what I can to help. That will keep me from being cold and cut off from others' suffering. I know they might use the money I give them to drink. I make them promise they won't, and if I don't believe them, I don't give. But ultimately, my reward is in the giving. What they do with the money is their responsibility.

Don't just give money; give clothes, furniture, and other items you no longer need. Many worthy charities survive primarily through these donations. Go through your closets once a year. If you haven't worn something in a year, you don't need it. Give it to someone who does.

Do It Yourself

You should do some things for yourself. Miss them, and you'll miss a blessing.

33 ■■ Enjoy Manual Labor

The whole long day of hard work had left on them no trace of anything but merriment.

—Leo Tolstoy

Background Any weekend gardener can testify to what Tolstoy, Thoreau, and others have said: manual labor is good for us. It's invigorating. It's healthy for our hearts, and it tones our muscles. It allows us to lose track of time and let our minds relax.

Manual labor is none too glorious for the coal miner or the day laborer, but for most of us who live sedentary lives and work primarily with our minds, it is beneficial for us. I enjoy chopping wood or building something. Tricia and I love to garden, and for this labor, we're rewarded with delicious produce!

There's nothing like manual labor to wring the stress out of my back and neck muscles. After a week of office work, I'm ready for the peace of some manual labor (and a long nap afterward!).

Action Find something you enjoy doing that works your muscles and leaves your mind free to wander. Life will make more sense after an hour or two of manual labor. And I promise you'll sleep better.

34 ■ Plant a Garden

Might I have a bit of earth?
—Frances Hodgson Burnett

Background If you have any space at all in your yard, a garden is one of the true joys of life. It's an outlet for occasional manual labor, yet it doesn't require too much. It saves money. The food you grow is better for you than food picked weeks earlier and shipped to the market. Most of all, the food tastes great. Home-grown corn or tomatoes are so sweet, you'll wonder if they're the same species as the store-bought varieties.

There's something almost mystical about having a garden. You put small seeds into wet earth, water them occasionally, and watch your work cooperate with God's creation.

Action This spring, plant a small garden. Find out what grows well in your climate. Ask your friends what they have grown. I personally think corn and tomatoes are the most rewarding because they come out so much tastier than the ones you buy. But so do peas, berries, and many other crops.

If you don't have much land, try growing a few things in pots. Herbs can even be grown indoors. Fresh herbs make any dish taste better than dry canned herbs.

35 ■ Find a Hobby

All work and no play makes Jack a dull boy.

—James Howell

Background Everyone needs a creative outlet. If you are always working, life is a bore. Very few people are fortunate enough to find an enjoyable creative outlet in their work. Even if you love your job, a hobby helps you avoid having all your waking thoughts consumed with work. You will have a broader perspective if you are interested in more than one thing.

A hobby should be something you love to do. It should be something that creates what some call a flow experience—you become so absorbed that you lose track of time, feel fully engaged, and perceive a deep sense of satisfaction.

Action If you already have a hobby that fits this description, make sure you give time to it. Don't fall into the trap of believing you must always be accomplishing something. And don't allow lesser activities, such as watching TV, to crowd out your hobby.

If you don't have a hobby, try a few things that attract you. Is there something you used to do that you gave up for lack of time? Is there something you always wanted to do—paint or learn to play the piano? Try it!

For some people, the perfect hobby is something they loved as children but stopped doing. As a young child, I liked to write stories. For some reason, writing was not reinforced by my schooling. I think it's because I liked to write stories on whatever came to mind; I didn't want to be told what I had to write about. Writing lost its pleasure for me until I rediscovered it a few years ago. I may or may not ever sell a story. Actually, I've never tried. The important thing is that I love to do it. It calls out something from my inner self, and it's worth doing for the sheer pleasure of it.

If you are stumped, ask your friends about their hobbies. Join with them and see if you enjoy theirs. If you're still stumped, just start trying things: grow some flowers, draw something, collect something, build a model, but do something!

36 ■ Do Simple Repairs and Maintenance

I like work: it fascinates me. I can sit and look at it for hours.

—Jerome K. Jerome

Background I was recently on top of my house running a plumber's snake down a vent pipe to try to fix a clogged drain. I'd already tried clearing the drain from inside the house, and I'd tried to find a way to get at it under the house. Nothing had worked. I had announced to Tricia that I would try one more thing—from the roof—then I'd call a plumber. It's not that it had taken me very long; it's just that I was getting frustrated. I thought my first efforts should have worked.

In five minutes, Tricia was yelling that the drain was clear. What a great sense of satisfaction I felt! It was not rocket science, mind you, but I had correctly diagnosed the problem and found the solution—and it was something I'd never done before. Tricia was proud of me. I had saved the cost of a plumber, and I had learned something new. And it took me all of twenty minutes.

Many repairs are actually very simple—replacing a washer in a faucet, clearing a drain, replacing a toilet valve, even fixing malfunctions in small appliances. It's very gratifying to fix something yourself. You simplify your life by saving money. And you often save time by not having to call a professional.

Employees of hardware stores are generally very helpful with almost any problem. They'll tell you if you really should hire someone. Or they'll explain to you how to fix it.

Action   Next time something breaks, give it ten or twenty minutes' effort before you pay someone else to fix it. You may still give up; that's okay. But see if you can learn to be a little more self-sufficient. In a few years, you may be an amateur plumber, carpenter, auto mechanic, and appliance repair person!

Don't Do It Yourself

There are times to do it yourself and times to let someone else do it. Wisdom is in knowing the difference!

37 ◫ Hire Someone for Difficult Jobs

When the car falls on your leg, give up!
—My wife, Tricia

Background Some years ago, I was trying to fix the brakes on my car. I didn't really know what I was doing. A bolt was stuck. I pulled and pulled on the wrench—to no avail. I stuck a pipe on the wrench for more leverage. I was going to get that bolt out if it killed me! It nearly did. By the time I realized the car was falling off the jack, it was too late to pull my leg out. The car came down right on my outstretched leg. The story has a happy ending, though. The jack stands were almost exactly the width of my leg, and when the axle came to rest on them, the edge of the car had given me only a surface cut. My leg was not crushed.

That was a frightening lesson to me. I'm wiser now. I hire someone for the dangerous jobs and for the ones I don't know how to do.

I bought a new water heater last year. I had learned quite a lot about plumbing through making repairs. I was 90 percent sure I could install the new water heater by myself. I turned off the water supply and applied my wrench to the first coupling. It wouldn't budge. I tried everything—no luck. In the old days, I'd have spent half a day trying to get that coupling off, only to discover that the next one was frozen, too. I gave up after twenty minutes and called a plumber. I spent the day lounging with Tricia and felt every dollar I paid the plumber was worth it.

Action This suggestion is an extension of the previous one. Try to do things yourself, but set a limit. If it isn't working after ten or twenty minutes —if you can't figure it out or it's not going your way—give up. There are times when the wisest move you can make is to hire a professional. Call it an investment in simplifying your life.

Never work with dangerous things unless you know what you are doing. Don't tinker with natural gas or electrical wiring. Don't open the back of a television set. And don't put your leg under a car while yanking on a bolt!

38 ■ Don't Accumulate Expensive Tools

Man is a tool-using animal.
—Thomas Carlyle

Background I used to think that if I bought a tool, it didn't count in the cost of repair. After all, I would use that tool again and again. Unfortunately, that hasn't often been the case.

I've even used a home project to try to justify buying a tool that I thought would be nice to own. I almost bought a table saw. We needed bookshelves in our family room, and Mr. Fix It (that's me) thought he'd do it himself.

I began salivating over table saws in the hardware store while I calculated the cost of my materials. Luckily, I happened to receive a furniture catalog at the same time. I didn't realize how inexpensive wall units could be. For a little more than the cost of the materials, I could buy a beautiful wall unit that included drawers, cupboards, and other elements I'd never be able to build. "But I want a table saw!" I protested.

I was tempted to justify it without counting the cost of the table saw, but I realized that I couldn't be sure I'd ever use the saw again. I decided not to build it, and I am truly glad. I have never had another use for a table saw. The decision simplified my life greatly for the month it would have taken me to build the shelves. And we have a very nice wall unit instead of an amateur version that we'd probably want to give away by now.

Action Count the cost of the tools as though you'll never use them again. If it's a ten-dollar wrench, and it will save a sixty-dollar plumber's bill, by all means buy it. If you're thinking about buying a table saw and building bookshelves, reread my story!

39 ■■ Find the Right Person to Help

A friend in need is a friend indeed.
—English proverb

Background Do you know what your friends do when faced with repairs or maintenance? Do you know what skills they have? If you know someone who is great with cars, you are lucky!

The world was a simpler place when neighbors helped one another. I'd help you build your barn, and you'd help me tend a sick horse. If we always take our needs to a national chain store, our lives are very impersonal.

Even if you need to pay for services, wouldn't it be nice if you could have a relationship with the people who provide the service, if you got to know them so well that you trusted them implicitly?

Action Try getting help from your friends first.

If that doesn't work, try finding people you can get to know. A moonlighting auto mechanic charges less than half what you'd pay the shop where he works during the day.

Even if you live in a large city, you can develop relationships with professionals who moonlight, small business owners, or even the manager of a large shop. It will simplify your life if you can develop a network of people you can turn to when you need help, people you can trust.

Help other people in areas where you have skills. You must give if you hope to receive—that's one of God's built-in designs for life.

Get Closer to Nature

A few decades ago, most people worked on farms. Although it's nice to be free of the backbreaking labor and the uncertainty of nature, most of us miss the effects of the seasons, the long periods of working alone, and the joys of harvest. Perhaps worst of all, we are alienated from the land that sustains us.

40 ■■ Recycle

Let us never forget that the cultivation of the earth is the most important labor of man.

—Daniel Webster

Background The move to save the earth is a vital development. I needn't rehearse the alarming statistics related to ozone depletion, pollution, and garbage.

Recycling is a simple contribution every household can make to this cause. It doesn't take much effort. Many disposal companies now provide a separate bin for recyclable items. It's a shame if you have this service available and don't use it. For others, it's a little more trouble but worthwhile nevertheless. We in the U.S. have 6 percent of the world's population and use 35 percent of the world's resources. How long do you think that can last? And ask yourself, Is it fair?

Action Start this week to recycle. Separate the recyclable cans and bottles from your trash. If you aren't sure where to take them, just keep your eyes open. You probably drive past a recycling center every day. Or the local newspaper may list recycling sites and hours.

Watch for school newspaper drives. Giving your newspapers to them is a good way to recycle and help a worthy cause at the same time.

If you have a garden, start a compost pile. Fertilizer takes enormous energy, and the runoff pollutes streams and rivers. Composting is really quite simple.

You'll start feeling like a responsible world citizen when you realize that half your garbage is going to some good use.

41 ■ Buy with Sensitivity to the Rest of the World

Are we as willing to evaluate our living standards by the needs of the poor as we are by the lifestyle of our neighbors?
—Richard Foster

Background   Most of us don't think about how our consumption affects anything else but us. But occasionally, the harmful effects become the center of attention. One example is the use of pesticide and its effects on farm workers. Another is the issue of trade with South Africa.

We should think about the effects we have on the poor, but we should also think about animals and the environment. One issue that represents a success story is the destruction of dolphins to catch tuna. It took a little time for the tuna companies to switch to dolphin-safe methods. They were unwilling to change their methods until the public caught on. They finally decided that there were enough of us who cared. The tuna companies would not have changed their ways by themselves. There had to be enough people who would be willing to pay more for tuna caught by methods that didn't hurt dolphins. Thankfully, there were.

Action   Be a person who cares, and translate that caring into your buying decisions.

Buy products that don't have wasteful packaging. If the packaging is twice as large as it needs to be, look for another brand.

Avoid non-recyclable plastic and Styrofoam whenever possible. Every non-recyclable plastic bottle and Styrofoam cup you've ever used will still be sitting in the ground centuries after you're gone.

Look for the recycle insignia, and buy products made from recycled materials.

Be aware of the human cost of products. Avoid products from companies whose workers are mistreated.

Every small action adds up. An Ethiopian proverb says, "If enough spiders unite, they can tie up a lion." Never give in to the defeatist attitude that you can't make a difference.

42 ◼ Get Outside

For many years I was self-appointed inspector of snow storms and rain storms, and did my duty faithfully; surveyor, if not of highways, then of forest paths.
—Henry David Thoreau

Background My earliest memories are of walks in the forest behind our house. I have a foggy memory of coming upon a deep gully in the center of thick woods, and to be honest, I'm not sure if it really happened or was part of a dream. But I was in the forest often enough that the memories of trees and streams filled my mind even at three or four, and they remain decades later. I learned much about life through watching the seasons cycle and tadpoles turn into frogs.

It's not as easy to go outside as it is to sit indoors. For one thing, to go outside means to live at nature's temperature rather than the artificial climate we've created for ourselves. But we miss so much of life remaining indoors. A friend of mine lived in the woods in northern Maine for a year. It is one of the coldest regions in the United States, and she went for a walk outdoors every day year-round. If she can do that, surely the rest of us can get outdoors.

Action Take walks in your neighborhood, or if you have access to a park, that's better yet.

Go outside in the morning and watch the sun rise, or watch it set in the evening. The next time there's a full moon, go out and walk in the silvery light. Take someone you love—it's very romantic! Make hiking or camping a family outing. Teach your children about the local trees and wildflowers. Take up fishing.

Find *some* excuse to be outside. You'll find it will slow you down and help you live at a better pace of life.

43 ■■ Watch for Beauty

You can experience the whole world of beauty in a single flower.

—Henri Nouwen

Background As I entered the busy years of college and career, I lost my early fascination with nature. I was thirty years old before I rediscovered my sense of wonder. Until that time, I didn't know a pansy from a petunia, or a daffodil from an azalea. I was always too busy, too consumed with my big plans and my many worries to take time for such trivial things.

When we bought our first home, the yard was full of flowers. Every day I came home to some new flowers in vases around the house. I began asking my wife their names, and I enjoyed the fragrance of jasmine, narcissus, and gardenias. I began to notice the flowers in the yard, too, and I even took responsibility to fertilize them regularly and watch for pests.

I'm still learning to enjoy flowers, and I'm sorry it took me so long to appreciate them. But this isn't the only example of my insensitivity to beauty. I can still drive home, absorbed with thoughts about my work, and not notice the orange sky at sunset or the golden light on the mountains. I'm happy to say, however, that I do notice my surroundings more often these days.

I can train myself to watch for beauty. And when

I find it, it lifts my heart from its anxious musings and reminds me that there are eternal things in life far more important than my worries or frustrations.

Action Today, look for every example of beauty you can find. Look for it in the scenery around you. Look for it in artwork. Look for it in the faces of the people you pass on the street. Your life will be richer for it.

When you find beauty, thank God for it, and let it lift your spirits for a moment.

Love and Be Loved

Relationships are eternal. Why then is it so easy
to shortchange the ones we love and so easy to
overcommit our time to lesser priorities?

44 ∷ Put Your Family First

The happiest moments of my life have been the few which I have passed at home in the bosom of my family.
—Thomas Jefferson

Background There's a drama being acted out in millions of homes in America. A man works from early morning until late at night six days a week. He sees his children for an hour or two a day, and when he does, he's tired and cranky. As the years pass, his wife's resentment grows; she's raising the children alone. The children view their father like a distant king; he's in command, but if they stay out of his way, they won't bother him, and he won't bother them.

In another version, Mom diligently pursues her own career and leaves the awesome responsibility of raising her children to overworked teachers. Or she spends hours each day on community work, helping others at the expense of those who need her most.

This drama is a tragedy in the classic sense; the players are moved by forces they don't understand. And the children don't know families can be any other way.

One day, the teenagers rebel. There is no firm foundation within the home to weather the storm, and the family begins to disintegrate.

I know several families that have gone through great heartache from precisely this problem. They are not bad people—they sincerely believed they were good parents. Only after a teenage son began to use drugs or a teenage daughter got pregnant did they understand something was wrong.

It's a problem of priorities. Our society places too little value on raising children. "What do you do?" is a question many stay-at-home parents dread. In reality, nothing is more important than the relationship with the ones closest to us.

The belief that it's quality of time—not quantity —is wrong. Your family needs both.

Action Examine your priorities in relationship to your family. Even if you don't have children, do you spend adequate time with your spouse? Watching TV together doesn't count! Do you spend time interacting, having fun together, discussing significant issues?

If you have children, do you invest some of your time in things that are important to them—attending ball games or teaching them to ride a bicycle? Do you *know* what's important to them? Make it a project to learn what they are struggling with, what makes them happiest, and what their hopes are for the future.

As your life becomes simpler, invest more of your time with the people you love. It will pay life-long dividends.

45 ■ Become an Encourager

*I expect to pass through this world but
once. Any good therefore that I can do, or
any kindness that I can show to any fellow
creature, let me do it now. Let me not
defer or neglect it, for I shall not pass this
way again.*

—Anonymous

Background I started a new job once, and like
any new employee, I was looking for cues about
whether I was doing a good job. Was I catching on
as fast as the average new employee? Was I making any obvious blunders?

For months I received almost no feedback, except from one person. This one person told me
every time we worked together that I was doing a
good job, that I'm smart, that we worked well together. It was no act either; he was sincere. He
didn't hesitate to offer criticism either. The criticism was always helpful, and in the context of his
encouragement, it was most welcome.

I noticed that this colleague was very popular
within the company. Why then is it so hard to emulate his style?

I've tried to learn a lesson from this experience.
It takes conscious effort to be an encourager. I'm
too distracted and self-absorbed most of the time
to notice other people.

Investing in people will greatly improve the quality of your life. My encouraging colleague has as much joy in his life as anyone I know. Being an encourager doesn't take a lot of time; it takes the will to get your eyes off yourself and onto others.

Action   What goes around comes around, as the saying goes. It's certainly true with encouragement. If you want to be encouraged, try encouraging others.

It's easy to encourage someone. Just look for something good to say. Everyone has commendable qualities.

Tell your friends something you appreciate about them. Tricia made a list of her friends and wrote down the qualities she most appreciated about each of them. She liked them even more after she did it! She's taking the time to encourage each of them about their good qualities.

We get more satisfaction from being praised for character than for individual incidents. If someone told me she appreciated that I told the truth, that would encourage me, but if she told me she appreciated that I was such an honest person, that would feel even better. Look for praiseworthy character traits in people, and encourage them.

Be especially sensitive to people who are having a bad day. You may be inclined to be rude to people who are rude to you. That is especially true in the marketplace; they don't seem fully human in the role as grocery clerk, flight attendant, or gas station attendant. But say something nice to them, and watch them look at you in disbelief. If you see someone be rude to them, take the opportunity to counteract it.

Become an encourager, and watch it come back around to you.

46 ■■ Invest in Edifying Relationships

*A man of many friends comes to ruin,
But there is a friend who sticks closer
than a brother.*

—Proverbs 18:24 NASB

Background The word for "ruin" in the proverb above originally meant "broken into pieces." The proverb is saying, "Don't have too many friends. You'll be broken up into so many pieces that you won't have any friends."

Women get this idea better than men. In surveys, men commonly rate the desire for companionship as the greatest need in their lives. Yet most men by the age of forty have not one person they consider a close friend.

Early in adult life, we begin making attachments that will ultimately become lifelong friends. One of the biggest dangers in the twenties and thirties is that we will invest in too many people. We will be scattered among so many friends that none of the relationships will ever develop into the "friend who sticks closer than a brother."

Ten years ago, Tricia and I developed a close friendship with another couple. We enjoyed Jerome and Dorothy so much that we spent nearly every evening together. We followed that pattern for months, and we often felt guilty about all the friends we were neglecting. Some of our other friends complained; some just stopped calling. I wasn't sure whether we were doing something wrong, but I knew that the kind of friendship we were developing was rare, and I didn't want to let it slip away.

Ten years have passed, and although we aren't together every night—we no longer even live in the same city, in fact—we are certainly best friends for life. In the perspective of ten years, those evenings we spent together were an investment that paid off handsomely.

I now see that there is a principle here. We are finite beings. We can love everyone from a distance, but we can't develop close relationships with more than a few people. These special relationships require time, and we have only so much of it. We must focus our lives on the few people who can be our closest friends.

Even Jesus invested Himself in only twelve disciples. Of those, three were with Him in the most important moments. And there was one special disciple, John, called "the disciple whom Jesus loved."

Action Do you have any close friends, any friends who are as close as brothers? If so, invest in them as a very high priority, second only to the time you spend with your family.

If you don't have such friends, do you know people who are likely candidates? Invest in them! Find time to be with them. Look for ways to encourage them. Look for common interests, and seek to understand what makes them who they are—their hopes, their plans, their struggles.

Let marginal friends slide if need be. Be content to have two levels of friendship: close friends who deserve substantial personal investment and acquaintances who receive minimal effort. Don't let guilt drive you to be a person of many friends, broken into pieces by lack of focus.

47 ■ Love the Unlovable

The biggest disease today is not leprosy or tuberculosis, but rather the feeling of being unwanted, uncared for and deserted by everybody.

—Mother Teresa

Background As the last chapter discussed, we need focus in our relationships if we hope to have close friends. If we share our time with too many people, people will become draining to us. We will find we have little to give to anyone. And we'll go through life without close friends.

However, after building the foundation of close friendships, we don't want to build a fortress around our lives. We need to reach out and give from our abundance to those around us. Life will never be satisfying until we give to others. We need to give to people who are unlovable, those who most need our love and concern.

Tricia and I spent several months in Ethiopia at the height of the famine there in the mid-1980s. That still stands out as one of the highlights of our lives. We worked long hours struggling to get food to the starving masses. Our love for the people overcame all of the horrible conditions and the fear of disease.

The Ministry of Money, in Washington, D.C., organizes several trips a year for what it calls a reverse mission. People travel with them to the

Third World and assist in some program to help the poor. People on the mission consistently report that they receive more from the poor than they give.

Recently, I gave half a sandwich to a homeless person, who said with gratitude, "God bless you!" I was overwhelmed. He had invoked the blessing of the Creator upon me. I had come away with far more than I had given!

Action   Look for people you can touch in some way.

Be one of the first to meet the new neighbor.

Look for the unlovable ones. Befriend the child in the neighborhood the other children don't seem to like. Seek out the person in church others ignore, the one who doesn't dress like the other members.

Look for ways to help the needy. Give them something, or volunteer at a local food bank.

Stop and talk to the homeless person on the street. Many homeless people have said that the worst thing about their condition is the invisibility. People pass them all day and look right through them.

48 ⬛ Invite a Friend to Join You on the Pilgrimage

A true friend is one soul in two bodies.
—Aristotle

Background The simple life doesn't come easily. The world presses in on you with all its demands and complexity. Your obligations weigh on you. Some steps toward simplicity take courage. You risk being misunderstood for not going along with the crowd. For example, try telling people you don't have a TV, and watch the reaction!

A friend can help. You can struggle together, test ideas with each other, and hold each other accountable.

Action Talk to a friend about simplifying life. If the person seems interested, share this book. Make a commitment to work on these issues together.

Set a regular time to communicate. A friend and I write to each other regularly. When we lived in the same town, we had lunch together once a week.

Push your talk past the clichés, and learn to devote your time to the significant issues in your lives. And be sure to look for ways to encourage each other whenever you are together.

Easy Does It

We were meant to rise above the mundane and touch the sublime. Don't miss the good things in life: love, truth, beauty, art.

49 ■ Stop Seeking Perfection

To live is to feel oneself lost. He who accepts it has already begun to find himself, to be on firm ground.

—Søren Kierkegaard

Background We were not put on this earth to attain some standard of perfection. The Christian message is one of hope: I'm not okay, you're not okay, but that's okay. Jesus came to redeem us from our imperfection by living the perfect life in our place.

God wants us to seek His character and His presence, not some ideal of perfection. We do not hold our own children to some ideal standard that they must live up to. Rather, we want them to become fully themselves and to learn our values and character. So it is with God. Many have wasted their years striving to live up to imaginary demands of a cosmic dictator. But the Bible says God is love.

If we can release ourselves from believing God demands our perfection, can't we release ourselves from our own demands? Can we give ourselves permission to make mistakes and seek to learn from them? Can we take time to rest, content to let go of some things we had hoped to accomplish?

Action Seek the will of God, not some imagined perfect plan for your life. I don't believe God's will is a straight line. I think of it as a wide playing field. There are boundaries, but there's a lot of room to express your individuality and make your own choices.

Stop striving for your own standards of perfection. Allow yourself a few bad days here and there. A good friend of mine says, "If I have two hundred good days a year, I'll accomplish great things in my life." It's liberating to allow yourself to read a book and lounge around on a day when you just can't seem to get going. For us Type A personalities, this isn't easy.

Some of us have the freedom to vary our routine even at work. Being an intense worker, my favorite days used to be those where I closed my office door and filled my "out" basket. I finally learned to lighten up and to take walks among the people who work for me. Without exception, that always proves more valuable than anything I could accomplish in my office.

50 ■■ Go with the Flow

Poli, poli.
—Kenyan proverb meaning "Oh, well, that's life."

Background   Tricia and I went through some difficult trials for several years related to infertility. We fought against the problem, and were often frustrated and angry.

At the same time, we've had many blessings in our lives. My recent career change went so smoothly as to be almost uncanny. Surveying the last few years, Tricia said, "There are some things in life that just aren't meant to be. No matter how hard you try to make something happen, you are just beating your head against a door. Other things have the ring of inevitability about them. You take a small step, you start to slide, and before you have put out any effort, you've arrived where you wanted to go."

We talked about this idea for weeks. We decided it's one of the keys to enjoying life. The biggest challenge is to have the wisdom to know the difference.

I think this is a life-changing revelation for us. We're trying to be more accepting of what God sends our way. We're trying not to fight so hard to change our circumstances. We want to apply more wisdom, to learn to sense when we've encountered something we can't change. Last year, with very little effort on our part, we adopted twins. It was clearly something that was meant to be.

Action   What things in your life have you fought to change with little or no success? Are they just not meant to be? The apostle Paul spoke about his thorn in the flesh. We aren't sure what it was, but we know he asked God repeatedly to take it away. When it didn't go away, he learned to accept that God was sufficient for him anyway.

Accept that some things in life will never happen —no matter what you do. You can strive for them all your life to no avail, or you can embrace the reality.

Other things in life are just meant to be, and a little effort will bring them to pass. Rejoice in these things.

51 ## Keep Simplicity Simple

Simplicity may be difficult, but the alternative is immensely more difficult.
—Richard Foster

Background I said early in this book that simplicity is not easy. Sometimes we're wrestling with the deepest questions in life: Who am I? Why am I here? Sometimes we're going against the grain of our whole society. Occasionally, the family will have differing opinions on how we should handle something.

It's worth the struggle; the rewards are huge. And the struggle doesn't have to make us frantic. We can take it one step at a time. We don't need to do it all today. Simplifying our lives is like peeling an onion—one layer at a time.

All fifty-two suggestions in this book are only that: suggestions. They have worked for Tricia and me. Some will work for you; some won't. All of them cannot possibly be applied in a single week. It's probably wise to work on only one or two at a time.

Action Don't let your efforts at simplification complicate your life. Take it easy. Work at a reasonable pace.

Get help from family and friends. Don't go it alone.

Simplicity should be a source of joy. The first time you skip your favorite TV shows or drive to the recycling bin, you may not have a hilarious experience. But don't give up. You'll know deep inside if you're on the right track. You'll feel life is fuller.

And if something doesn't work for you, forget it and try something else. Don't get bogged down in your efforts to simplify.

52 ■■ Follow Your Bliss

Let what you do arise out of who you are
. . . whatever I do the rest of my life, it
will not be in order to have an identity. It
will be the result of allowing my God-
given self to emerge.

—Stan Mooneyham

Background The great philosopher Joseph Campbell summed up his advice to people in this simple phrase: follow your bliss. In it he found the accumulated wisdom of centuries of mythology, fables, and stories.

To follow your bliss means to trust your instincts about what is right for you. That doesn't mean you should ignore morals and conventions, but within the basic framework established by God and society, find the unique path meant for you.

As I said earlier, I believe that if we pray for God's help and seek His character in our lives, we have a wide field to play on. I don't view God's plan for each of us as a razor's edge. One slip and we've left the straight line forever? No, it's not like that.

As we become mature, the choices that are right for us become the ones that give us joy. The deepest part of ourselves, the part created in God's image, yearns to come to the surface. It takes years to clear away the clutter and learn to follow our instincts. But it's worth it. We will not be led astray.

Action   Learn to follow your instincts as you depend on God.

Cultivate your interests. If a subject appeals to you, learn about it. If you enjoy something such as art, seek it out.

Find those things that bring joy.

You can't begin to discern these instincts until you have a simple life. Those who spend every moment surrounded by noise or stimulated by television and those who ceaselessly strive to accomplish will never discern them. Simplify your life, and then follow your bliss.

Stephen J. Woodworth was formerly vice president for marketing at World Vision, the renowned relief and development organization. He is now a management consultant with the Thomas Group, specializing in improving the competitiveness of all types of businesses. He lives with his wife, Tricia, and their two children, Heather and Joel, in Poulsbo, Washington.